ALTERNATOR
BOOKS™

BREAKTHROUGHS IN
DEEP SPACE
SCIENCE

Wil Mara

Lerner Publications ◆ Minneapolis

Lerner Publications Company
A division of Lerner Publishing Group, Inc.
241 First Avenue North
Minneapolis, MN 55401 USA

For reading levels and more information, look up this title at www.lernerbooks.com.

Main body text set in Aptifer Sans LT Pro Regular 12/18.
Typeface provided by Linotype AG.

Library of Congress Cataloging-in-Publication Data

Names: Mara, Wil, author.
Title: Breakthroughs in deep space science / Wil Mara.
Description: Minneapolis : Lerner Publications, [2019] | Series: Space exploration
   (Alternator Books) | Audience: Ages 8–12. | Audience: Grades 4 to 6. | Includes
   bibliographical references and index.
Identifiers: LCCN 2018016813 (print) | LCCN 2018025128 (ebook) |
   ISBN 9781541543713 (eb pdf) | ISBN 9781541538733 (lb : alk. paper)
Subjects: LCSH: Space astronomy—Juvenile literature. | Space sciences—Juvenile
   literature. | Technological innovations—Juvenile literature. | Outer space—
   Exploration—Juvenile literature. | Deep space—Juvenile literature.
Classification: LCC QB136 (ebook) | LCC QB136 .M37 2019 (print) | DDC 523—dc23

LC record available at https://lccn.loc.gov/2018016813

Manufactured in the United States of America
1-45056-35883-7/26/2018

Contents

A NEW PLANET

Proxima Centauri is the next-closest star to Earth, after our sun.

About 4.2 **light-years** from our sun is a star called Proxima Centauri. Scientists discovered it in the early twentieth century. In August 2016, scientists also learned that a planet **orbited** Proxima Centauri. They called the planet Proxima B. It is the closest **exoplanet** to our solar system. It is similar in size to Earth, and scientists thought it may have water and even life.

Scientists studied the area around Proxima B with a huge telescope in Chile called the Atacama Large Millimeter/submillimeter Array (ALMA). Scientists at first thought that more planets might be around Proxima Centauri. But a large flare erupted from Proxima Centauri in 2017. The flare likely gave off dangerous **radiation** that could cause any water on the planet to evaporate and damage any **atmosphere** or life Proxima B might have. Scientists also determined it was unlikely that other planets orbited the star.

The universe is full of mysteries, and scientists are making discoveries every day about the stars, planets, and other objects beyond our solar system. Scientists want to learn more about the universe and to develop new ways to explore the most distant regions of outer space.

ALMA, the telescope used to learn about Proxima B, was built in the Andes mountains of northern Chile. This kind of equipment works best in high, dry areas.

LYING BEYOND

For thousands of years, people have gazed up in wonder at the night sky.

Have you ever looked into the night sky and wondered just how far you could go into outer space? Humans have been curious about the universe for thousands of years. Scientists use telescopes and spacecraft to explore the planets and moons of our solar system. But space extends far beyond the solar system, and scientists want to explore all of it.

EARLY EFFORTS

In 1972 NASA launched *Pioneer 10*. This spacecraft became the first to reach Jupiter and send images of it back to Earth. In 1973 *Pioneer 11* launched to take pictures of Jupiter and Saturn. Both spacecraft continued traveling through space and sending information back to Earth long after they passed the planets. They studied particles from the sun and other types of energy in the outer solar system. NASA lost contact with *Pioneer 11* in 1995 and with *Pioneer 10* in 2003. Though their scientific instruments no longer work, both spacecraft are still flying through space.

Pioneer 11, shown with Saturn in 1979 in this artist's impression, was named for its eleven scientific instruments.

Both *Voyager* probes included a phonograph record of music and nature sounds. If aliens find it, they can learn about humans on Earth!

The Voyager program, begun by NASA in August 1977, had even more success than the Pioneer program did. NASA launched two **probes**—*Voyager 1* and *Voyager 2*—to study Jupiter, Saturn, Uranus, and Neptune. After flying by these planets, the probes continued toward interstellar space—the regions between stars in space—beyond the edge of our solar system. In August 2012, *Voyager 1* became the first spacecraft to enter interstellar space, 11 billion miles (17.7 billion km) from the sun.

Voyager 1 sent information to Earth about this region of space, including how particles from the sun interact with particles from other stars. Meanwhile, Voyager 2 sent back information about the environment at the edge of the solar system. As of 2018, the probes were both still working and exploring space.

Since the *Voyager* probes' flyby of Jupiter, scientists have learned much more. This image from 2016 shows a bluish aurora, a light show in the planet's atmosphere.

STEM FOCUS

The scientific instruments on the *Voyager* probes are powered by a type of **atom** known as an isotope. It gives off heat that powers a generator, which produces energy. The isotope gives off less heat as time passes, so it produces less power. To conserve power, scientists began turning off the scientific instruments. The last ones will likely stop working in the 2020s. But the probes may drift through space for thousands of years.

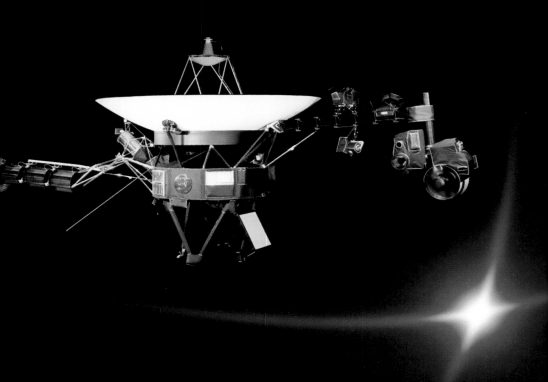

CHAPTER 2

SEEING INTO SPACE

Radio telescopes can pick up radio wave information. That includes data from stars, planets, galaxies, and dust clouds.

Spacecraft that can travel beyond our solar system are expensive to create and difficult to maintain. It also takes a long time for a spacecraft to travel so far. Scientists estimate that it would take a spacecraft tens of thousands of years to reach the next closest star to our solar system. So scientists use powerful telescopes to explore distant regions of space.

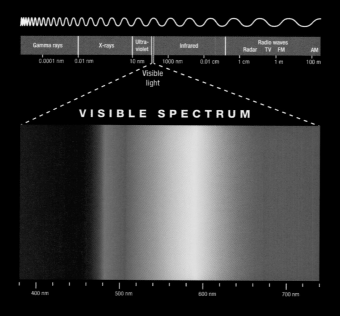

Gamma rays | X-rays | Ultra-violet | Infrared | Radio waves
Radar TV FM | AM

0.0001 nm | 0.01 nm | 10 nm | 1000 nm | 0.01 cm | 1 cm | 1 m | 100 m

Visible
light

VISIBLE SPECTRUM

400 nm | 500 nm | 600 nm | 700 nm

The electromagnetic spectrum includes all kinds of energy.
This diagram shows only the colors of energy we can see.

ELECTROMAGNETIC SPECTRUM

Scientists need different types of telescopes to look deep
into space. This is because objects such as stars give off many
different kinds of energy in waves that travel through space.
The light we can see is just one kind of energy. Other kinds
include radio, infrared, ultraviolet, and X-ray. The entire range
of energy is called the electromagnetic spectrum. Different
types of telescopes pick up different types of energy.

Some of these powerful telescopes are on Earth, such as ALMA, the radio telescope that studied Proxima B. But Earth's atmosphere interferes with electromagnetic waves from space. To get a better look, scientists began launching telescopes into space.

ALMA was built at an altitude of 16,570 feet (5,051 m) above sea level. It's higher than most of Earth's atmosphere.

The Hubble telescope captured this image of the remains of a star that exploded about eight thousand years ago.

SPACE TELESCOPES

In 1990 NASA launched the Hubble Space Telescope. The telescope orbits 340 miles (547 km) above Earth and observes space through ultraviolet light, visible light, and near-infrared light. Hubble has made more than one million observations.

Scientists used information from Hubble to learn more about the size and age of the universe. In 2018 scientists announced that Hubble had spotted the most distant star ever seen. The star, nicknamed Icarus, is so far away that its light took nine billion years to reach Earth.

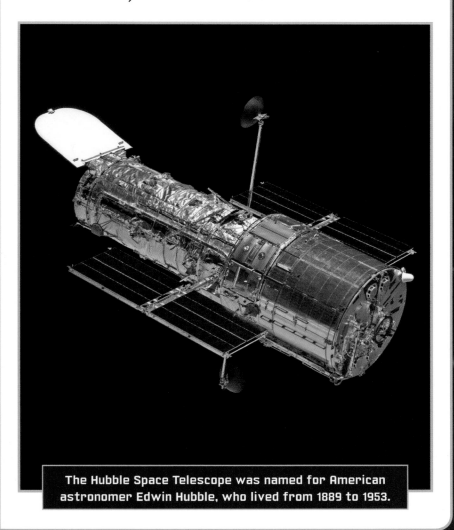

The Hubble Space Telescope was named for American astronomer Edwin Hubble, who lived from 1889 to 1953.

The Spitzer Space Telescope launched in 2003. It was the first telescope to detect light from a planet outside our solar system. The infrared telescope created a map of the spiral structure of the Milky Way galaxy, and it has found several exoplanets. In 2016, with the help of the Transiting Planets and Planetesimals Small Telescope (TRAPPIST) in Chile, Spitzer confirmed the presence of seven Earth-size exoplanets 40 light-years away.

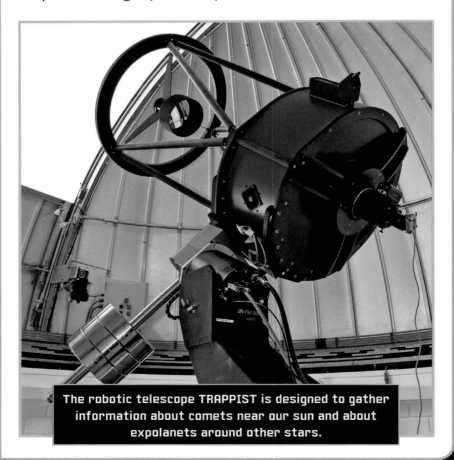

The robotic telescope TRAPPIST is designed to gather information about comets near our sun and about expolanets around other stars.

The TRAPPIST-1 system is named for its star, TRAPPIST-1. Its closest planet orbits the star in 1.5 Earth days. This artist's impression shows what the surface of one of these planets might be like.

Scientists continued studying these planets, known as the TRAPPIST-1 system. They used Hubble, Spitzer, and the Kepler Space Telescope, which has found more than two thousand exoplanets since its launch in 2009. Researchers say that the seven planets are rocky and may have water. Scientists want to continue studying the planets' atmospheres and learn whether they may be able to host life.

CHAPTER 3

BLACK HOLES

This artist's impression shows a black hole surrounded by debris from a torn-apart star.

Along with observing distant stars and exoplanets, NASA's space telescopes have helped scientists discover and understand black holes. A black hole is an area of space with **gravity** so strong that nothing—not even light—can escape. Scientists believe black holes form when a star collapses. Black holes are invisible, so no one has ever actually seen one. But we can observe the effect they have.

The strong gravity of black holes pulls on nearby objects. By observing these objects, scientists can find black holes. Some black holes shoot out jets of **matter** and energy. Radio telescopes and Hubble can capture images of these jets. Black holes also produce X-rays. The Chandra X-ray Observatory is a space telescope designed to observe these waves of energy.

This image from Chandra shows jets coming from a black hole in the Centaurus A galaxy, about 12 million light-years from Earth.

Chandra was designed to find very hot matter and gas, which can come from explosions, strong gravity forces, or magnetic fields.

CHANDRA X-RAY OBSERVATORY

Chandra launched in 1999 and began observing galaxies, stars, and black holes. Scientists designed the telescope to operate for five years, but the telescope is still sending information and images to Earth. In 2017 Chandra captured the deepest-ever X-ray image of space. Scientists say the image shows thousands of black holes.

Chandra has also observed black holes closer to home. It has been watching an area in the center of the Milky Way galaxy since it launched. This area contains a huge black hole known as Sagittarius A*. It is about 26,000 light-years from Earth. It is the largest known black hole in the Milky Way and the closest black hole of this size.

In 2018 scientists said evidence from Chandra shows that several more black holes may be near the center of the Milky Way. These black holes are much smaller than Sagittarius A*. Scientists predict that up to ten thousand of them may be in the galaxy.

Sgr A*

The labeled blue circle shows Sgr A*, short for Sagittarius A*. The rest of the circles show areas that scientists think might contain other black holes.

LOOKING AHEAD

Planetary-imaging scientists used data from *New Horizons* to create this color-enhanced view of Pluto.

NASA has sent one more spacecraft beyond the planets of our solar system. Launched in 2006, *New Horizons* reached the dwarf planet Pluto in 2015. The spacecraft sent the first-ever close-up photos of Pluto to Earth. Then it traveled beyond Pluto and farther into the region of space known as the Kuiper Belt. *New Horizons* is heading for a small, icy object 4 billion miles (6.4 billion km) from Earth known as MU69. NASA scientists hope that information about MU69 will help them understand more about how objects in space form.

EVENT HORIZON TELESCOPE

Although it is impossible to capture an image of a black hole, scientists hope to get a better glimpse at the event horizon—the area around a black hole. Because black holes are so far away, a telescope with enough power to get a clear image of an event horizon would need to be the size of Earth. So scientists use eight radio telescopes to act like one Earth-size telescope. They point all the telescopes at the same part of the sky at the same time and combine the information to create one image. This network is known as the Event Horizon Telescope.

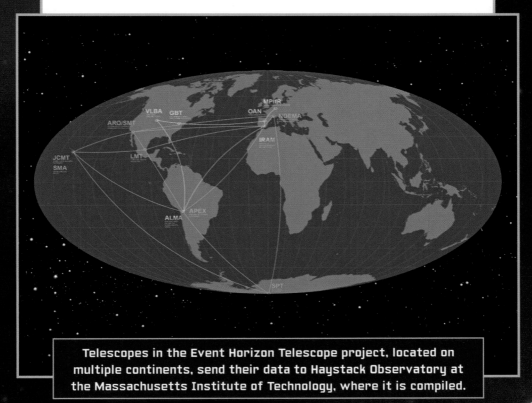

Telescopes in the Event Horizon Telescope project, located on multiple continents, send their data to Haystack Observatory at the Massachusetts Institute of Technology, where it is compiled.

In 2017 scientists used this telescope to observe two black holes. In 2018 they began to analyze and combine the information that might reveal the first-ever image of an event horizon. The Event Horizon Telescope project is ongoing, and scientists hope to gather new images of the two black holes each year.

The James Clerk Maxwell Telescope in Hawaii, shown here with a comet called Hale-Bopp, is a contributor to the Event Horizon Telescope project.

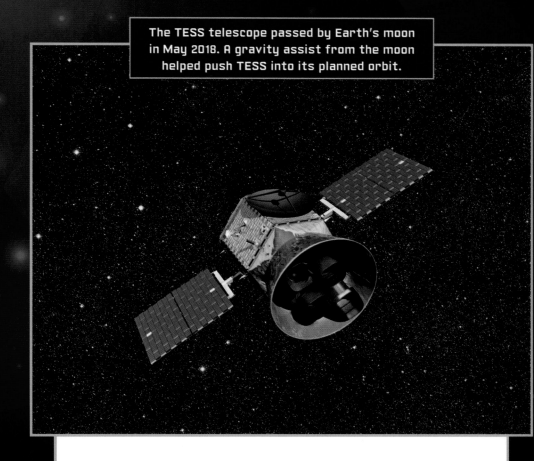

The TESS telescope passed by Earth's moon in May 2018. A gravity assist from the moon helped push TESS into its planned orbit.

SCANNING THE SKY

In April 2018, a new space telescope launched. The Transiting Exoplanet Survey Satellite (TESS) will work for two years to observe the entire sky. Its four cameras will focus on the two hundred thousand brightest stars near our sun to look for evidence of exoplanets. Scientists will study the images to find small dips in the brightness of these stars. This happens when a planet passes between its star and Earth. Scientists will be able to find exoplanets and learn about their size and orbit.

Will the Webb telescope discover life in deep space?

NASA also plans to launch the James Webb Space Telescope in 2020. This telescope will orbit the sun from a spot 1 million miles (1.6 million km) away from Earth. The telescope will use its cameras and scientific instruments to observe the exoplanets found by TESS. The Webb telescope will gather photos and information about the history of the universe, formation of galaxies, and life on other planets.

STEM FOCUS

The Webb telescope will observe galaxies that are over 13 billion light-years away. Many telescopes use mirrors to collect light from objects in space. The larger the mirror, the more detail the telescope can see. The mirror on the Webb telescope will be bigger than any telescope mirror that has ever gone to space! The mirror will have eighteen segments that can fold up to fit inside a rocket and unfold once the telescope is in orbit.

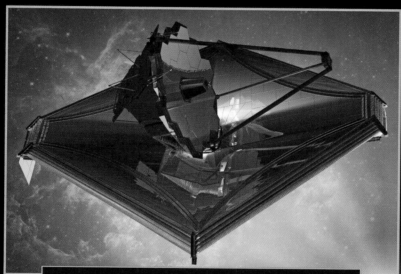

A thin layer of gold covers the telescope's mirror segments to help improve light reflection.

The Hubble telescope captured this view of the Pillars of Creation, part of an area called the Eagle Nebula, in which new stars are forming.

Scientists will continue to study information from spacecraft and telescopes to learn more about the universe. They are also developing new technology with updated cameras and scientific instruments. The future is sure to be full of incredible scientific breakthroughs in deep space.

WHAT THE TECH?

More than one hundred scientists around the world are working together to operate the Event Horizon Telescope and analyze the information it collects. The radio telescopes in the network are in Hawaii, Arizona, Spain, Mexico, Chile, and the South Pole. To collect accurate information, the telescopes must all point to the same place at the same time. And the skies must be clear in every location. Once the information is collected, scientists will send it to two locations where computers will combine it into a single image. Then scientists will analyze the image.

Cold, dry air and 24-hour winter nights make Antarctica's South Pole Telescope perfect for gathering data about outer space.

GLOSSARY

atmosphere: a layer of gases that surrounds a planet

atom: the smallest particle of an element that can exist on its own

exoplanet: a planet orbiting a star that is not our sun

gravity: a force that draws particles or objects together

light-years: units of length that measure the distance light travels in one year

matter: all substances that contain atoms and take up space

orbited: traveled around a body in space, such as a star or a planet. The curved path around an object in space is an orbit.

probes: tools or devices used to explore things, such as planets

radiation: energy that moves in invisible rays or waves

FURTHER INFORMATION

Deep Space
http://kidsahead.com/subjects/15-deep-space

ESA Kids: Our Universe
https://www.esa.int/esaKIDSen/OurUniverse.html

Hamilton, John. *Hubble Space Telescope: Photographing the Universe.* Minneapolis: Abdo, 2017.

Kids Astronomy: The Universe
http://www.kidsastronomy.com/deep_space.htm

Kruesi, Liz. *Finding Earthlike Planets.* Lake Elmo, MN: Focus Readers, 2018.

NASA Kids' Club
https://www.nasa.gov/kidsclub/index.html

Roland, James. *Black Holes: A Space Discovery Guide.* Minneapolis: Lerner Publications, 2017.

Scott, Elaine. *To Pluto and Beyond: The Amazing Voyage of* New Horizons. New York: Viking, 2018.

INDEX

Photo Acknowledgments

Image credits: NASA/ESA/Hubble Heritage Team, pp. 4, 14, 28; ESO/B. Tafreshi/
twanight.org, p. 5; Westend61/Getty Images, p. 6; NASA Ames, p. 7; NASA/JPL, p. 8;
NASA, ESA, and J. Nichols (University of Leicester), p. 9; NASA/Hulton Archive/
Getty Images, p. 10; Haitong Yu/Getty Images, p. 11; PeterHermesFurian/Getty
Images, p. 12; ESO, pp. 13, 16; NASA, pp. 15, 20, 26; ESO/N. Bartmann/spaceengine.
org, p. 17; ESO/ESA/Hubble/M. Kornmesser, p. 18; ESO/WFI (visible)-MPIfR/ESO/
APEX/A.Weiss et al. (microwave)-NASA/CXC/CfA/R.Kraft et al. (X-ray), p. 19; NASA/
CXC/Columbia Univ./C. Hailey et al., p. 21; NASA/JHUAPL/SwRI, p. 22; ESO/O.
Furtak, p. 23; David Nunuk/Science Photo Library/Getty Images, p. 24; NASA/ESA/
Hubble/Davide De Martin, p. 25; NASA/Northrop Grumman, p. 27; Eli Duke/Flickr
(CC BY-SA 2.0), p. 29.

Design element: filo/Getty Images.

Cover image: NASA/JPL-Caltech/R. Hurt (SSC).